Walks on the High Fells

Conisto…
and G… mere

by
Tom Bowker

Dalesman Books
1988

Key to Maps

a summit

a road or walled lane

a tarn and beck

a lake

woodland

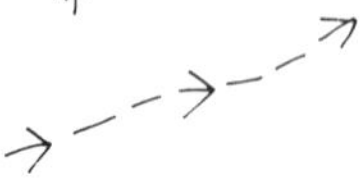

a footpath with direction arrow

a building

a bridge

a wall or fence that is particularly useful for navigation

cairns, caves, natural landmarks, passes and points of interest

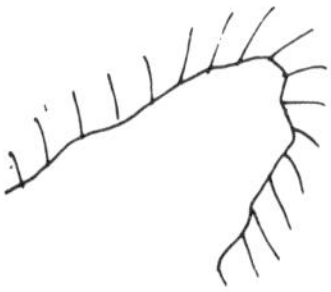

crag, quarry, precipitous slope

Printed by Swannack, Brown & Co. Ltd., Hull, England

Contents

Cover Map by Barbara Yates
Sketch Maps by Helen Bowker

The Dalesman Publishing Company Ltd.
Clapham, via Lancaster, LA2 8EB.

First published 1988

ISBN: 0 85206 943 X

Introduction

I HAVE over the past few years been writing a series of booklets covering walks in various areas of Lakeland under the general title of 'Walks from your Car'. They are principally aimed at the more leisurely inclined fellwalker, or the family party, and the distances involved and the terrain covered reflect this. I've been delighted with their reception and hope this first book of a series aimed largely at the more serious fellwalker will be equally well received. It will be obvious from the mileages and/or the heights of ascent that the bulk of these walks are made of sterner stuff, at times requiring considerable energy and resolve. They should be treated with due respect. Boots should be worn and rucksacks should contain waterproofs, spare clothing, map, compass, whistle and survival bag.

In winter a torch, balaclava, mittens and some extra food should be added. When snow and ice coat the fells, an ice-axe should be carried. Crampons are becoming more commonly used by fellwalkers, and rightly so. Frequent practice in the use of map and compass make that winter day when their use suddenly becomes vital much less terrifying. Remember the cardinal rule - start using your compass from a point where you know where you are, don't wait until you are lost. Successful navigation through deteriorating conditions adds a bonus to your day and a boost to your confidence. Remember, in an emergency, all becks flow downhill and if followed with care can be fast escape routes in bad weather. Never be afraid to turn back. The fells will still be there next weekend.

Alongside each walk, save the 'marathon', is a sketch map to be used in conjunction with the text. It is advisable, however, also to carry the relevant sheet of the 1:25000 The English Lakes Outdoor Leisure Maps. All the place names in the text refer to the 1982 edition of these maps. The mileages and heights of ascent are approximate. Parking details are as per the maps, local authorities and tradition up to press, but are always liable to change.

The only way to learn about the fells is to be out regularly in all conditions. There will be times when you are frightened and times when you are physically exhausted. Ironically, these are the days that live most vividly in the memory and when you learn most about the mountains. Don't forget that it's a game, it's fun, it's adventure. For the fellwalker, given reasonable fitness and equipment, using his/her commonsense, the dangers are more apparent than real. Statistically, you are probably in more danger in your home or on your journey to and from the fells.

The Lakeland fells have become inextricably woven into the weft of my life. My addiction to climbing them led to love, marriage and fatherhood, and innumerable friendships. They stimulated my interest in writing and are the bedrock of its continuing development. They have given me untold days of rewarding physical endeavour, good company, and wonderment at the beauty seen. If this booklet should bring such pleasures to any who read it I will be content. Happy walking!

Tom Bowker

March,1988

CONISTON

Walk 1 **8½ miles**
2500 feet of ascent

South of Walna Scar

An enjoyable outing over peaks rarely thronged with walkers. Especially good for wildlife, flowers and Lakeland's industrial history. Harder than the humble height of the peaks would suggest.

Parking: From Torver, follow the road to Broughton-in-Furness. About a mile from Torver turn right up a steep minor road. When plantations appear on your right continue to a Forestry car park and picnic site on the edge of the trees, giving a fine view of the Duddon estuary. (GR 253927).

CROSS the fence by a stile and follow a path which at present descends the edge of a felled area to debouch on to a forest road. Turn left to a junction. Turn right and follow a forest road over and down to where a stony path slants sharply down to your left. Follow this down to and across a concrete bridge over the Appletree Worth Beck. Continue uphill past a shed to emerge on to another forest road. Turn left and follow this road as it twists downhill until it passes between an old wall standing in the trees on either hand. To check you are in the correct spot, look down the bank on your left for a footbridge over a beck.

Turn right just beyond the wall up a path often churned into bog by forestry vehicles or blocked by felled trees. Keeping parallel to the old wall, follow this path over and down to emerge on to a forest road. Turn right to shortly see a path veering down to your left. Follow this down, passing an old shed, to a gate leading on to a tarmac road. Turn right and follow the road to cross the River Lickle over humpbacked Water Yeat Bridge. Climb up the road towards Stephenson Ground Farm. Caw, crowned by its man-like cairn, offers a shapely challenge ahead. More distantly to your right, White Pike's surprisingly rugged profile thrusts above the headwaters of the Lickle.

BEYOND the first building at Stephenson Ground, follow a 'Walna Scar' sign through a gate on your right, then turn left behind

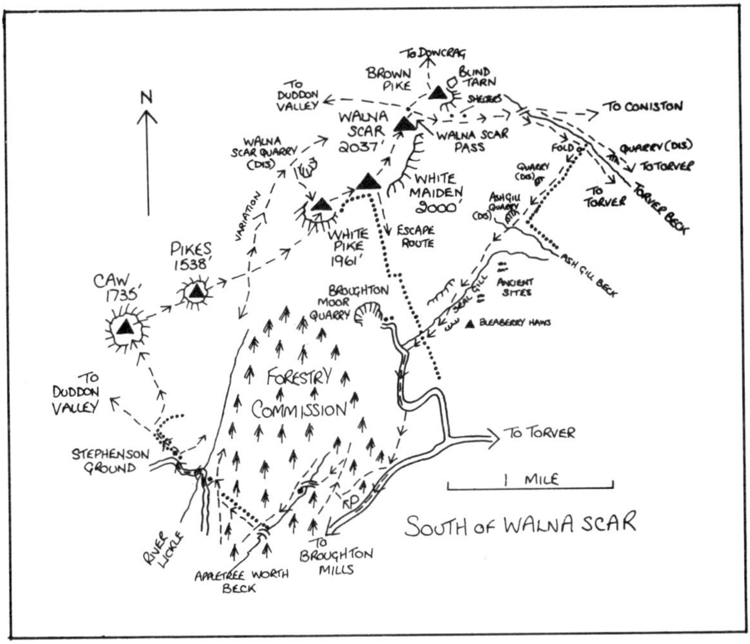

the farm buildings to climb a grassy path alongside a wall. This eventually climbs between walls to a gate leading on to the open fellside. Follow a path to the right for a short way until a faint path veers left into a boggy gap. This path then intermittently appears as it roughly follows the upper reaches of the Broadslack Beck towards the trig point. The final slope is steep and liberally banded with rock. The view from the top is extensive, and particularly nicely detailed in the north-west to north-east arc, from Devoke Water round to Coniston Old Man. Fell-spotters should look for an unusual view of Yewbarrow, above and beyond Burnmoor.

Now head north-easterly, down then up, along an intermittent path, to 'bag' the lower but ruggedly shaped peak plurally and prosaically christened Pikes. Beyond the next dip, White Pike throws up surprisingly steep and craggy defences for a fell which from most angles looks like a dull grassy spur. Now head down into the dip below. cross the brideway linking Stephenson Ground and Walna Scar, and climb up towards a grassy ledge slanting leftwards under an obvious overhang. Climb steeply up the ledge and the fellside above to emerge on to a delightful ridge leading to the summit cairn of White Pike.

An interesting alternative is to turn left in the dip and follow the bridleway round to the disused Walna Scar Quarry. This path is indistinct and boggy at first but improves into a built-up quarry track as it curves around the fellside. The quarry is extensive and as you explore upwards a high narrow fissure leads you into a huge man-made pit where a 'gurt' cavern gapes evilly in a corner. A lasting memory of this quarry is coming virtually face to face with a fox as I stepped out of the rift. The fox didn't appear perturbed and drifted lazily but lissomly up the steep spoil, pausing frequently to give us an interrogative stare before vanishing amongst some piled boulders. If you contemplate exploring the cavern remember time and weather wreak slow but sure havoc on the shattered slate of old quarries.

Retreat back through the fissure and climb right, along the rim of the quarry, before slanting right, up steep grass, to emerge near the White Pike cairn. (Every time Carolyn, a friend of mine, climbs a fresh summit over two thousand feet she sticks a gold star on the appropriate spot on a map of Lakeland hanging in the office where she works. A 'gold star' has the significance of a 'munro' for Carolyn and has become a byword amongst her walking friends.) Despite all your efforts so far on this walk you still have to bag a 'gold star'.

To do so, head east-north-east into a dip, where a wall climbs up from the right, and follow this wall to shortly reach the cairn crowning White Maiden 2000 feet, and a sudden view of Coniston Water. The wall turns down to the right here, providing a good escape route in bad conditions. Now head north-east along a broad undulating grassy ridge to reach the small cairn on Walna Scar 2035 feet, overlooking the pass of that name. Drop down into the dip and turn right down the well-worn and stony track. Walna Scar was a vital link in the mesh of ancient trading and travelling routes draped across the Lakeland fells. Probably a prime purpose of this route was to serve the extensive quarries hereabouts. Lower down you may spot a small stone edifice to the left of the path. It is similar to ones found under Nan Bield Pass which Wainwright suggests were shelters for travellers caught out by darkness or bad weather.

Continue down to the iron-railed stone bridge spanning the Torver Beck. From here look back into the great corrie behind Coniston Old Man to see the baroque and darkly-cloven splendour of Dow Crag. Do not cross the bridge, but turn down a path following the right bank of Torver Beck. Just before the path passes through a gap in a wall, near a sheepfold, turn right along a faint path along the foot of the slope, some distance from the wall but parallel to it. Soon the path improves and the view ahead opens up, to reveal the ruined workshops of Ash Gill Quarry. Beyond these the skyline dips between a rounded hill, Bleaberry Haws, and a rugged ridge rising towards White Pike. This dip is your objective.

At the ruin, the wall on your left turns away. Walk through the ruins to cross Ash Gill Beck below a cascade. Now head up either bank of Seal Gill towards the dip. Path traces are faint and intermittent. Small cairns and hollows on the left bank are dignified as 'sites of antiquity' on the 2½" map. It must have been a bit parky up here with only woad long-johns between you and the Helm Wind!

Go through the dip and down to where an obvious grassy ramp leads up on to the left bank of the gill. Follow this down to find a stone stile in a wall. This wall is the 'escape route' from White Pike previously described. Cross the stile and walk down to join a tarmac strip serving the unsightly collection of sheds nestling in a gaping wound of ripped slate and heaped waste that is the working Broughton Moor Quarry. Turn left up the tarmac. When it curves left near some posts leave it and turn right, across the moor, towards the corner of woods. Beyond a boggy dip, a built-up path leads up to a stile near the corner of the wood. Cross it and turn right up the road to your car.

Walk 2 **14½ miles**
4500 feet of ascent

The Coniston Two-Thousands

What I would nowadays call a longer and more strenuous than average day. Nevertheless, a splendid 'bag' of ten, or possibly eleven, 'two-thousand footers', virtually all of it ridge walking of the highest order.

Parking: The car park in Coniston behind the church. (GR 304975)

WALK up the lane to the right of the Black Bull Hotel. The tarmac deteriorates into a rough track climbing above the cascades of Church Beck. At the entrance to Coppermines Valley a bridge signposted 'Coniston Old Man' spans the beck. Ignore this and walk on to where a path forks right up the fellside to swing left above and behind a terrace of refurbished miner/quarrymen's cottages. Overlooking the derelict workshops and extensive spoil heaps of the Coppermines Valley, itself a former mines path, it gives delightful walking. In the nineteenth century around six hundred men and boys were employed in the network of mines and quarries of which this valley was the hub. Sufficient ore was produced annually to warrant the railway being brought to Coniston in 1859. Thrusting above the ravaged valley Coniston Old Man and Brim Fell curve protective ridges around high cupped Low Water. The eroded 'tourist' route to the Old Man climbs the left hand ridge, whilst Raven Tor, leading to Brim Fell, appears largely neglected.

Your path leads to an impressive old mine building, looking more like a Afghan fort, guarding the entrance to the high combe of Red Dell. On the banks of the Red Dell Beck, where it begins its tumble out of the combe, are tunnels and fearsome fenced off shafts; also pits of dressed stone in which spun great water wheels pumping water out of the deep levels. The constant problems of flooding levels, the attraction of cheap foreign imports, the switch from copper-bottomed hulls to iron ships, all contributed to the demise of Lakeland copper mining.

Cross the beck and climb on to the crest of a rubbly old tramway slanting up the fellside and follow it to its end just below a mine shaft. Then climb left and right to emerge on to the crest of a ridge overlooking Levers Water. Climb northwards up this ridge, following

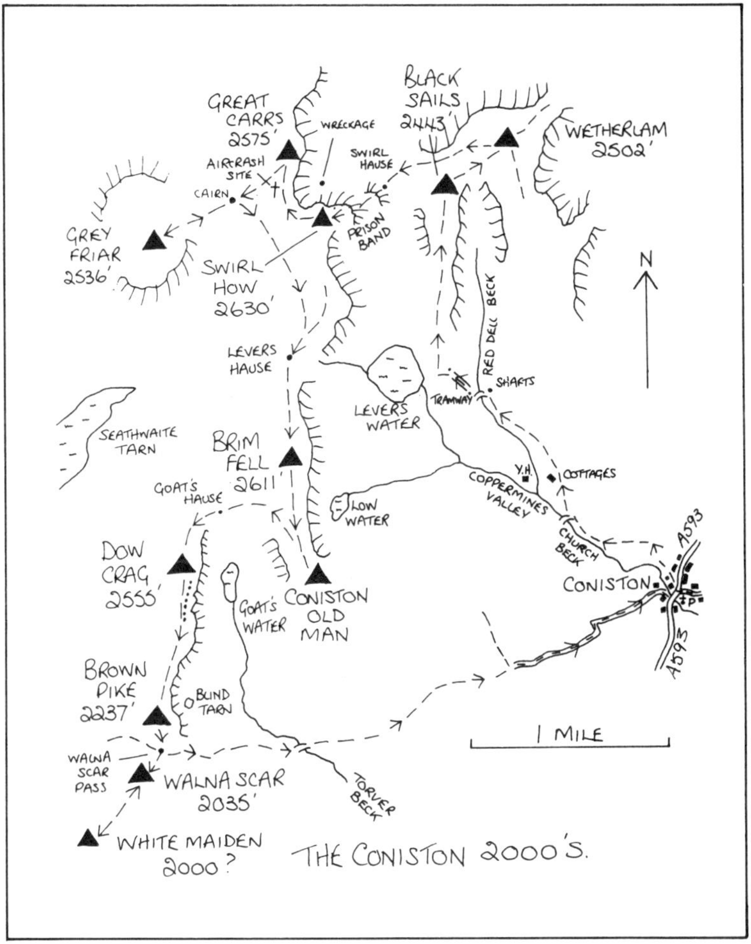

a faint path twisting around rocky outcrops, to reach the summit of neglected Black Sails, 2443 feet. One down, ten to go! Now head north-east, across Red Dell Head Moss, to reach the rocky summit of Wetherlam, 2502 feet. Leave Wetherlam and head west-south-westerly along the eroded path clinging close to and occasionally edging over the rim of the steep flank falling into Greenburn, ending in a stony descent on to the narrow saddle of Swirl Hause.

Climb south-westerly out of Swirl Hause up the curiously-named

Prison Band ridge to reach the handsome cairn perched on the airy prow of Swirl How, 2630 feet. Descend westerly before swinging north around the grassy and frequently windy rim of Broad Slack. Peer over the rim to spot the wreckage of a Halifax bomber that struck the summit ridge of Great Carrs whilst returning from a bombing raid over Europe and disintegrated, with the loss of its crew. As well as a large section of the mainframe there are propeller mountings and engines, one wedged in the bed of a beck, scattered about the combe. As you climb up to the summit of Great Carrs, move left to spot a wooden cross set above piled wreckage on a patch of still scorched earth marking the scene of impact. Framed against the majestic backcloth of the Scafells, it makes a dramatic and moving picture. Whatever one's personal opinion about either the evils or necessity of war, it's hard to continue your climb without reflecting that our freedom to roam these fells we love was hard won by such sacrifices. From Great Carrs, 2575 feet, head west-south-westerly down easy grass on to Fairfield, the broad saddle below Grey Friar. A steepish climb soon eases off on to the grassy outcrop-studded dome of Grey Friar, 2536 feet. A neglected outlier of the Coniston fells, it offers a splendid view into Upper Eskdale and the ring of delectable peaks guarding the Great Moss, the heartland of mountain Lakeland.

Return to the Fairfield saddle then bear right, south-easterly, along a faint path traversing across the grassy western upper flank of Swirl How to emerge on to the eroded path scarring the central ridge just above Levers Hause. Descend into the saddle and climb southwards up its farther slope to eventually level out on to the broad grassy dome, crowned by a handsome cairn, of Brim Fell, 2611 feet. Continue southwards into a dip before the final climb up to the trig point, cairn, and stone platform-crowned summit of Coniston Old Man, 2631 feet, the monarch of the Coniston fells . With seven down and four to go, retrace your steps a short way to where a path turns left, north-westerly, slanting across steepening grass, above the dark gleam of Goat's Water, before turning west and down on to the broad saddle of Goat's Hause. Now climb in a steep curve leftwards, south, over increasingly rocky ground, to reach the great block of volcanic ash that forms the summit of Dow Crag, 2555 feet.

On one stormy ascent of this fell we 'chickened-out' of the climb to the crest of the summit block for fear of being hurled on to the boulders below it. As we'd approached from the south a brutal wind had frequently shoulder-charged us painfully to our knees, whilst bellowing and taunting us to dare to move closer to the crag rim.

Descend south along the ridge, alongside an old wall at first, to where a great wedge is bitten out of it. This is the rim of Great Gully, and a circumspect peek over gives some idea of the height and steepness of the crag. A little further down the ridge, from the rim of Easy Gully, a safer aerial view may be had of climbers in action on the crag's 'A' and 'B' buttresses. Beyond Easy Gully the crag tails off and the flank falling away to your left, though steep, is largely grass and scree. Below now nestles Blind Tarn, so named because it has no exit beck, and, following Levers Water, Greenburn Tarn, Seathwaite Tarn, Low Water and Goat's Water, the sixth lovely upland tarn to be overlooked on this walk. A somewhat larger 'burp' in the ridge brings you to the summit of Brown Pike, 2237 feet, before dropping again to meet the eroded path crossing the summit of Walna Scar Pass.

Cross this path and climb up the grass slope beyond to shortly reach the small cairn crowning Walna Scar, 2035 feet. According to the cartographers of the latest 2½" map this is your last two-thousand footer in the bag and it's now downhill all the way. Older 1" maps, however, claimed that the dull summit of exotically-named White Maiden, crowned by a cairn near a wall corner around a quarter of a mile further along the ridge, just peeked over the two thousand foot contour. When you have given it the benefit of the doubt, or not, return to the Walna Scar path. Turn right and follow it down to an eventual junction with a tarmac road that leads you to a steep finish down into Coniston.

Your soles may react painfully to the impact of the last mile or so of tarmac. Ignore them by gazing over the hedgerow to your left where the greater part of the lovely humpety-bumpety skyline you have just traversed is painted gloriously upon a Lakeland sky. Consider the warm glow inside your boots the righteous one of a job well done.

Walk 3 **9 miles**
4300 feet of ascent

Steel Edge and Raven Tor

Searching for a different approach to Wetherlam and the Old Man one winter day I finished up with this. The considerable loss of height and subsequent re-ascent in the middle section may make you wince, but just get your head down, grit your teeth, count steps, or whatever you do on 'steep bits', and keep saying to yourself "it's doing me the world of good". They tell me it's character building and, anyway, if you're a Lakeland fellwalker who fancies his or her chances 'Munro-bagging' you'll have to get used to this sort of thing. It's a far from boring walk giving new insights on possibly very familiar fells. Try it.

Parking: Tilberthwaite, on the parking space below the old quarry spoil heaps. (GR 306009).

CLIMB the spoilheaps by the path signposted 'Tilberthwaite Gill'. As you climb turn into the third (or is it fourth?) opening on your left to inspect a huge quarry pit. Return to the path and follow it to a fork. Take the left fork climbing high above Tilberthwaite Gill before swinging right past an old mine entrance. Shortly it swings left alongside Crook Beck, where it forks. Take the right fork, cross the beck, and follow a path rightwards towards the base of an obvious spur thrusting out of the rugged flank of Wetherlam. When the base of the spur is reached climb where convenient on to its broad crest and follow it until the angle eases on to the elegant grassy Steel Edge. This abuts steeper rockier ground where pleasant easy scrambling leads ultimately on to the broad south-south-easterly ridge of Wetherlam and a junction with the popular path, which is now followed towards the right to the summit cairn of Wetherlam, 2502 feet.

Descend south-westerly across Red Dell Head Moss and up on to the summit of apparently infrequently visited Black Sails, 2443 feet. Now comes the 'daft bit', the eleven hundred foot descent down the fell's south ridge to the weir in the Levers Water dam, where Levers Water Beck spills forth. Cross the weir on to the dam. It's a well-constructed piece of work, its flat grassy top ideal for picnicking and sunbathing, and the boulders of its facing as diving platforms. On a boiling day fairly recently I was coaxed into 'skinny-dipping' into

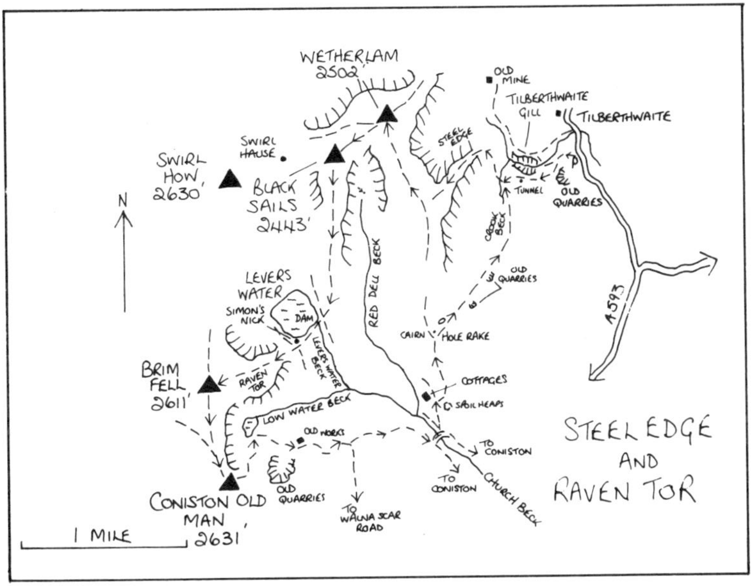

these chilling but refreshing waters. I feel that 'podgy-dipping' is a more accurate description of our middle-aged antics!

The steep rocky spur of Raven Tor, thrusting out from the main Old Man-Swirl How ridge, towers above the south-western end of the dam. To reach it, follow the crest of the ridge behind the dam to arrive at a grassy saddle below Raven Tor. From this ridge there is a fine view of yacht-speckled Coniston Water and the wooded hills of Furness rolling away towards the distant blue line of the Pennines and Ingleborough's pronounced hump. To the right of this ridge is the fenced-off chasm of Simon's Nick, reputedly a thousand feet deep. Simon was said to be in league with fairies who, in return for his trust, revealed to him hidden reefs of copper. When he betrayed their trust they caused him to be buried in this horrendous hole. Out of the depths of fenced-off shafts below and to the right of the saddle I have had the bizarre sight of vapour venting into the chill surface air of a winter day. Also around here, though I've yet to spot it, is reputedly the remains of a goose-bield, or antiquated fox trap. A dead goose was hung from the end of a plank delicately balanced over a deep stone circular enclosure. The weight of the fox lured by the bait was sufficient to tip plank and Brer Fox into captivity - and ultimately a dire fate.

Climb up steep grass to the foot of the rocks and pick your own way through them. Some grassy grooves around to the right offer the easiest line. The crest of Raven Tor is a delightful walk, largely grassy, which broadens as it merges into the fell proper. The final climb leads you on to the grassy summit dome, where a short walk left brings you to the fine summit cairn of Brim Fell, 2611 feet. It's now an easy walk south, along a broad and boot-scarred ridge, to the trig-point, cairn and stone platform crowning Coniston Old Man, 2631 feet. Old Man could stem from the Norse *alt maen*, meaning 'tall hill', or from either of the local meanings of 'tall cairn' or 'early miner'. Perhaps the last is most apt, for surely few other Lakeland peaks have been for so long rent and gnawed by man. When I was a raw mountain-mad lad it was the highest mountain in Lancashire, and boasted a height of 2635 feet on my 1948 one-inch map. Now it's a modest Cumbrian fell, forty odd places down the list, and has had four feet lopped off! I know thousands have climbed it since 1948, but surely even they couldn't wear away four feet of volcanic ash.

Captain Joseph Budworth, a one-armed veteran of the siege of Gibraltar, and author of a best-selling book about Lakeland, is given credit for the first recorded ascent, in 1792. It was supposed to be a rest day, and he had strolled from Ambleside merely to look upon Coniston Water. The sight and challenge of the Old Man proved too much and, sustained by nips from his brandy flask, he made it to the top and back to Ambleside - some rest day!

Descend the 'tourist' route past Low Water and through the extensive old quarry workings. Where the rough quarry track makes its last twist right, south, to ultimately link up with the Walna Scar path, you fork left down a grassier path. This slants above Coppermines Valley to reach the footbridge spanning Church Beck. Cross the bridge and turn left then shortly right up a path climbing the fellside behind a terrace of refurbished old miner/quarrymen's cottages. At a fork turn right, towards spoil heaps, then almost immediately left to climb steeply into a narrow gap, Hole Rake, at the foot of the south ridge of Wetherlam. This ascent is part of the popular path to Wetherlam. From the gap, descend a fine built-up former quarry path, passing a cairn where the Wetherlam path forks left and a small reedy tarn. Small derelict quarries are passed on your right, a beck is crossed above a waterfall, before your outward route is rejoined at the path fork alongside Crook Beck.

Walk 4

8 miles
2850 feet of ascent

A Greenburn Horseshoe

Not a long walk but a delectable one over shapely peaks giving widespread views. It is perhaps the varied and visible reminders, from huge man-made caverns, old mine buildings, and wrecked warplanes, of mankind's impact upon the fells that makes this walk particularly unique.

Parking: Take the minor road, marked 'Cumbria Way' on the 2½" (South West) map, (GR 329023), branching west off the Skelwith Bridge-Coniston road, the A593. It forks immediately it leaves the major road. The left-hand fork heads for High Oxen Fell Farm. The right fork passes the farms of High Park and Stang End before crossing a bridge over a beck, then shortly reaching a 'Ford' (2½") and footbridge over the River Brathay. Park either on the right-hand grass verge just beyond the bridge over the beck or close to the ford. The ford/footbridge can be reached from Little Langdale village by a narrow rough lane signposted 'Tilberthwaite Ghyll'. After a traumatic crossing in a Mini packed with panicking teenage daughters and friends I don't recommend attempting the ford! (GR 316028).

FOLLOW the path past the bridge and alongside the river. After passing through a gate, slate spoil heaps will be seen to your left, and shortly afterwards a gate leading up into them. Go through this gate and climb up to the second terrace and a hut with a National Trust emblem on its door. Behind the hut is a rocky fissure crowned by a slate arch. Pass under the arch and follow the fissure (do not be deterred by the low wet tunnel seen ahead), until a hidden opening on the left leads to a dramatic view into a huge man-made cavern supported by a thick leaning pillar of slate, now commonly known as 'The Cathedral'. (Since my first visit years ago there's been a rock-fall into the fissure which has to be climbed over in order to view the cavern. The cavern is magnificent but obviously there is possible danger from falling rock). Should you be feeling adventurous, when you emerge from the fissure turn left and a short climb brings you to the rim of the huge quarry pit where you may see parties of youngsters being taught to abseil. From a corner to your right a steep scrambly path leads into the piled boulders in the quarry bed and another closer glimpse into the Cathedral. A further short scramble leads down into a lower pit where a walk through a short tunnel leads you into the floor of the cavern and to the base of the great pillar.

Return down to the original path and continue. After passing Low Hall Garth Farm and a climbing hut the path climbs between walls below slate spoil heaps to a gate leading on to the open fellside. Follow the path beyond, passing a seat, to a fork. Continue along the right fork to a second fork. Take the left fork which leads you to the derelict workshops of the Greenburn Lead Mine, seen about a mile ahead. Away to your right, rising above the hollow cupping Blea Tarn and framed between Pike O'Blisco and Lingmoor, the Langdale Pikes display themselves to rugged effect. The Greenburn ruins are extensive, with one grim, body-wide and poorly fenced shaft which is in my reference files for the day I write my Lakeland who-dunnit. Higher up the valley the old mine reservoir is a pleasant bathing and picnic spot, given the weather.

Your objective now is the crest of Wetherlam Edge, high above to your left. To reach it climb initially up an old 'sledgate' zig-zagging right and left up the fellside. Although it is drawn on the 2½" map the start of this path is not too obvious. Climb left above the main spoil heaps to a smaller spoil heap below a flooded shaft. Slant right from here to find the 'sledgate'. Once found, it gives pleasant walking up an otherwise rough and steepish fellside. Its original purpose was far from pleasant. The early miners and quarrymen used to shift up to a quarter of a ton of ore or slate in sleds, or trailbarrows, running before them like a horse, then laboriously hauling the empty sled back uphill, possibly up to fifteen or more times a day. Little wonder that a travel writer of the time described them as appearing 'wan and worn, as if they were all consumptive or had heart disease'. The 'sledgate' ends near a tunnel mouth. Now the way becomes a little rougher and steeper. Climb left to a spoil heap. Climb its left edge to a further tunnel. Climb to the left of this up a line of cairns to emerge on to the crest of the ridge and a well-worn path, close to a pronounced hump of rock. Now turn right and climb the steepish rocky ridge known as Wetherlam Edge to emerge onto the summit of Wetherlam, 2502 feet.

From Wetherlam, head generally west-south-westerly along the eroded path clinging close to and occasionally edging over the rim of the steep flank falling into Greenburn, ending in a stony descent which leads on to the narrow saddle of Swirl Hause. En route energetic peak baggers might feel inclined to nip south to 'bag' Black Sails, 2443 feet. Climb south-westerly out of Swirl Hause up the curiously-named rocky Prison Band ridge to reach the handsome cairn perched on the

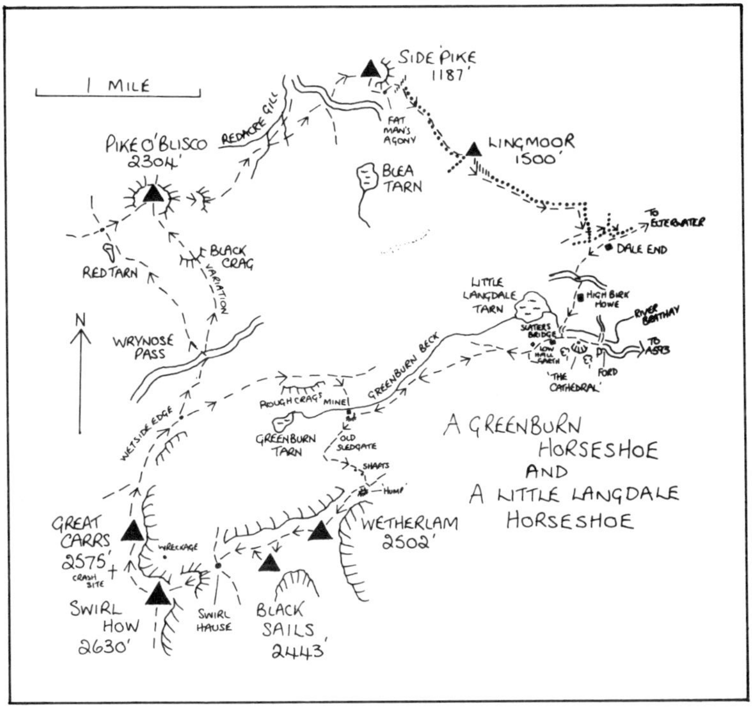

airy prow of Swirl How, 2630 feet. Descend westerly before swinging north around the grassy, and frequently windy, rim of Broad Slack. Peer over the rim to spot the wreckage of a Halifax bomber that struck the summit ridge of Great Carrs whilst returning from a bombing raid over Europe and disintegrated, with the loss of the crew. As you climb up to the summit of Great Carrs, move left to spot a wooden cross set above piled wreckage on a patch of still scorched earth marking the scene of impact. (Read Walk 2 for more details). The view from Great Carrs is very fine. Easterly, Wetherlam rises massively out of the depths of Greenburn. Southerly, Dow Crag thrusts a spiky contrast to the dome of Coniston Old Man. Far westerly, if you are lucky, you may spot the Isle of Man floating serenely upon a shimmering sea. It is north-westerly, however, where my eyes are always drawn, where the Scafells lord it over the shadowy bowl of the Great Moss, the heart of mountain Lakeland.

Descend north over the subsidiary summit of Little Carrs, virtually following the precipitous Greenburn rim of the fell, then down stony ground rightwards on to the ridge of Wetside Edge. The angle eases and the ground becomes easier underfoot as the ridge widens and gradually curves eastward around Greenburn. At the foot of Wetside Edge, a cairn marks a path fork. The left fork slants down to ultimately join the motor road crossing the crest of Wrynose Pass. You continue with the ridge path. Beyond Rough Crags the ridge narrows, steepens, and becomes a little rockier. Once below the steep bit leave the path and bear right down easy brackeny slopes towards the ruins of Greenburn Lead Mine now almost immediately below you. Cross the Greenburn Beck near the mine to rejoin and return by your outward route.

Shortly after leaving the mine, before you reach the gate in a wall, move left to the edge of the beck for a glimpse of a fine waterfall. A little lower down you may spot a cave entrance at the base of the far bank. This is reputedly where Lanty Slee, a local whisky smuggler, once worked his illicit still. Shortly after passing Low Hall Garth Farm, a stone stile in the wall on your left leads to the lovely Slater Bridge, a must for photographers and worth the little detour. Should you be blessed with a heatwave, there are splendid bathing pools both up and downstream of the bridge.

Walk 5 **11 miles**
4800 feet of ascent

A Little Langdale Horseshoe

This walk absorbs the peaks of the Greenburn Horseshoe and shares others with the Great Langdale Horseshoes. Tougher than the former and less well known than the latter, it contains many splendid aspects of both. The ground tackled is always interesting; caves, quarries, tarns, cascades and crashed warplanes are bonuses; and the scenic feast is a gourmet's.

Parking: As for Walk 4.

FOLLOW the instructions given in Walk 4 as far as 'At the foot of Wetside Edge a cairn marks a path fork'. Take the left fork and follow it down to steep grassy zigzags leading on to the motor road crossing Wrynose Pass. Cross the road and climb north-westerly up the path leading to and past austere Red Tarn. According to Postlethwaite's classic 'Mines and Mining in the English Lake District' iron ore was delved around here. The worn sanguine grooves of the adjoining paths hint at the presence of iron. Recently an analysis of pollen accumulated in the silt of tarns was carried out in Lakeland. Red Tarn, at 1850 feet, was the highest to be investigated. The conclusion was that before the advent of the Neolithic axe men this now bleak gap between Pike O'Blisco and Crinkle Crags was once covered by forest. From the saddle beyond the tarn, an important path junction, you are faced with the view featured on the front cover of the best selling 'Fellwalking with Wainwright'. The craggy ramparts of Crinkle Crags echelon away towards rock - armoured Bowfell.

Turn right on the saddle to climb the path leading up to the rocky trench dividing Pike O'Blisco's two summits. Scramble left to the slabby highest point, at 2304 feet. An interesting alternative route from Wrynose Pass is the fell's south-east ridge. It's mainly grassy but there are a couple of craglets to explore en route, with a Napes Needle look-alike under Black Crag. Leave Pike O'Blisco by either of two paths bearing left, easterly,out of the rocky trench. Both have 'scrambly bits' through the belts of rock guarding the summit. They merge on easier ground beyond and bring you to the rim of Redacre Gill. Follow the eroded path down the left bank of the gill but just beyond where it crosses the beck look for a path forking right. Follow this path, traversing across the fellside, to emerge onto the minor motor road linking Great and Little Langdales at its highest point near a cattle grid.

Cross the road, climb a stile over a wall, walk past a stone memorial seat, and climb the path up the south-west ridge of Side Pike, 1187 feet. Side Pike's ascent is worth the effort for the detailed view of the famed Langdale Pikes, ranging round from the tiered rock cone of Pike O'Stickle to the pale underbelly crags of Pavey Ark. Beyond the cairn, the ground falls abruptly away and unless your name is Icarus, or should I say especially if it is, retrace your steps a little way. A path forks left then slants further leftwards to the foot of a rocky ridge. Move around the corner to find a rock finger at the base of a slightly leaning crag upon which there are some hard rock climbs. Squeeze behind the finger - what old timers would call a 'Fat Man's Agony'. Beyond this, follow a wall, first right side, then left side, to reach the cairn crowning Lingmoor, 1538 feet, where Windermere's glimmering waters leap immediately into view. Did you know that from here, given a clear day, Blackpool Tower can be picked out just below and to the left of Wetherlam?

Beyond the cairn, cross the stile over the fence then head south-easterly along the broad undulating ridge with a fence or wall always to your left. About half a mile on, approaching a wall corner, the path turns steeply down to the right to meet a crossing valley path near a wall corner. Turn left along this to shortly emerge onto a rough track above Dale End Farm. Turn right, passing the farm, and down to reach the Little Langdale-Wrynose Pass motor road. Turn left. Very shortly, turn right up the farm track to High Birk Howe Farm. Pass the farm entrance, go through a gate, and follow a steepening path down alongside a wall to reach the lovely Slaters Bridge spanning the infant River Brathay. As you descend, to your right Little Langdale Tarn reflects the delectable frieze of fells you have just traversed. Should there be a heatwave, fine pools above and below the bridge offer a refreshing dip. Cross the bridge and the wall stile beyond and turn left back to your car.

Walk 6 **6 miles**
2800 feet of ascent

Harter Fell, Mediobogdum and Dunnerdale

Harter Fell is an elegantly sculpted and isolated fell that is more of a mountain than others half its height again. Hardknott Castle (Mediobogdum) adds a flavour of history and romance to the walk, whilst Dunnerdale is as lovely, and only half as crowded, as any other Lakeland valley.

Parking: In the Dunnerdale Forest car park and picnic site a few hundred yards north of where Birks Bridge spans a foaming Duddon. (GR 235995).

CROSS the Duddon by the less elegant bridge near the car park. Follow a forest road, passing through a gate and gradually climbing leftwards. Where this road emerges from the trees a track branches left down to the buildings at Birks. Continue with the forest road which passes through a gap in a wall. Just before reaching the gap bear right up a path climbing the bank near a red-ringed marker pole. Follow it through a gateway into a boggy dip where paths fork. Bear right to climb up between trees. When the trees close in ahead, look for a cairn in the trees to your left marking a path. The way bears upward to the left now, either in the bouldery bed of an incipient beck or in the trees to its left. Both merge in a more open area to the left of a small crag. A

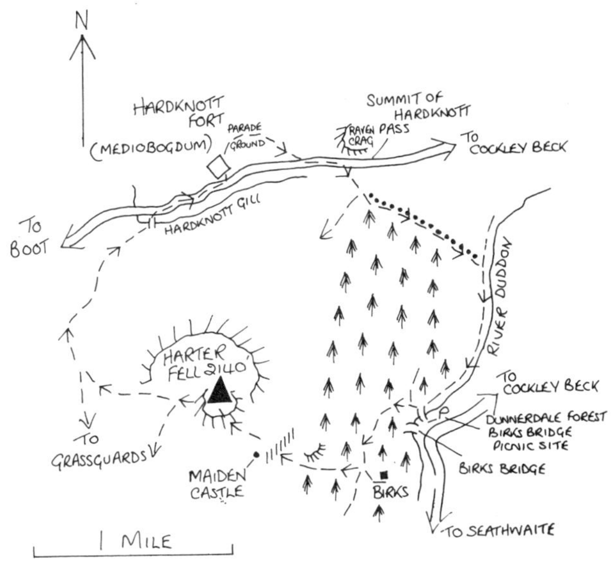

HARTER FELL, MEDIOBOGDUM, AND DUNNERDALE.

little higher the path goes to the left of another crag and emerges onto the open fellside.

A prominent rock pinnacle, Maiden Castle on the large OS map, crowns the skyline ahead and the path crosses a stile over a fence to the right of it. Now the angle eases but the path becomes fainter if anything. It has a tendency to bear to the left of most of the rocky outcrops approached before eventually bearing right up to the summit. It doesn't really matter if you lose the path for this is an isolated peak and as long as you keep heading upwards you are bound to reach the top.

Scramblers will find their fun keeping to the rock that thrusts generously through the grassy pelt of this fell and will be delighted when they reach the top. This is a great block of Borrowdale Volcanic, towering to the east of the faint-hearted trig point and making Harter

Fell one of the rare Lakeland tops that can only be bagged by use of the hands as well as the feet.

The highlights of the view from Harter Fell are, for me, both to the north. Immediately below, Mediobogdum straddles its spur, commanding Eskdale. You're gazing upon the archetypal structure of the Roman fort that remained unchanged for centuries and was planted on conquered soil from Persia to Perthshire. Now raise your eyes from a crumbling symbol of man's ever-violent history to the timeless magnificence of England's highest and wildest hills.

Now follow a path down a grassy groove to the left of the trig point. This north-of-westerly path is well worn, being the most popular way up and down the fell, albeit the most boring. Ignore a cairned diversion left shortly below the top. Continue down slanting rightwards, with Eskdale spreading away below, to reach a gate signposted 'Bridlepath /Hardknott'. Beyond this the path is wide and obviously built up and it leads easily down to the foot of Hardknott Pass. Skirting Harter Fell, linking Eskdale to Dunnerdale, it was once part of the network of roads that shuttled goods, animals and people across mountain Lakeland. Ahead, Bowfell, the quintessential mountain shape, towers elegantly above Upper Eskdale.

Walk up Hardknott's corkscrewing grass verges to explore Mediobogdum. Although the actual ruins are not particularly impressive it must be one of the most dramatically situated military strongholds in the world. Surely the most hard-bitten legionary, or auxiliary, must have been impressed by the view from the ramparts as the seasons draped it in their coat of many colours. It was built and garrisoned by a cohort (around 600 men), of Dalmations (Jugoslavs, not dogs!), who doubtless frequently cursed the Lakeland weather as they drilled on the parade ground they had painfully constructed out of the intransigent fellside above the fort. (In his book 'Fell Days' the late Graham Sutton offers the amusing idea of bored off-duty Roman soldiers timing each other with water clocks up climbs on nearby crags).

Follow the line of the old road curving under the crags of Border End to meet the tarmac road higher up. Climb this to a point just past the steep buttress of Raven Crag and beyond a culvert. Here a path branches off to the right. Follow it over a rise and through a gap in a wall before veering right, through a gap in another wall, to reach the corner of a plantation. Go down a soggy path between a wall and the trees. When the trees turn away, continue down between the wall and a fence to the bank of the Duddon. Turn right and follow the river bank to reach the bridge back to the car park.

LANGDALE

Walk 7 **9½ miles**
2900 feet of ascent

Esk Pike and Bowfell from Cockley Beck

Esk Pike is a fine fell which suffers by standing in the shadow of Bowfell, a yet finer fell, and also by rising above Esk Hause, the Piccadilly Circus of mountain Lakeland. It is often seen therefore, merely as an energy-sapping obstruction on a traffic-congested highway from one to the other. It deserves better treatment. From the North, from Dalehead or the minor summits of Barrow or Barf, it is a thrusting, ruggedly isolated fell. Close to, from Rossett Pike, especially in winter garb, it rears a steep cornice-crowned flank above the deep bowl of Angle Tarn. Climb out of the Cumbrian Badlands up the fell's long south ridge, especially in winter, and you will quickly realise that this badly maligned fell has much to offer.

Parking: On the grass verges (not the passing places) of either the Wrynose or Hardknott Pass roads near where they meet at Cockley Beck Farm. (GR 247017).

WALK up the Hardknott road to where a path leads right into Mosedale. Initially the path is excellent, but in the upper dale it deteriorates rapidly into a swamp. To anyone with experience of Lakelands's several 'mossy' dales this should be no surprise. We usually veer leftwards up the fellside to escape the worst on the outward leg, but slosh straight through on the return. The Scafells beckon enticingly ahead, however, and the view from the saddle at the dalehead of the wild hinterland beyond, the Cumbrian Badlands, is worth a bootful, or two, of damp feet. To the north-west the Scafells, together with Broad Crag and Ill Crag, rise out of the shadowy bowl of the Great Moss, scree-fan, crag, pinnacled ridge and high combe all piling skyward on to an excitingly cleft crest. Immediately below you lies the basin of Ling Cove, dominated by the elegant pyramid of Bowfell and the western crags of Crinkle Crags. It has to be admitted that set amidst this glamourous crew Esk Pike does look a bit dull. It is easy to see why being ignored appears to have been this fell's lot in life.

It was not named until 1870, and until the 1960's was not even allowed the dignity of this name on the popular maps. It had to be content with a dot and the not unimpressive figure of its height.

Drop down to the bank of Lingcove Beck, crossing the Brotherikeld-Three Tarns/Ore Gap path en route. Cross the beck and climb up towards the rocks of Pianet Knott, the first of many rocky 'burps' on this lengthy ridge. If every one was assiduously climbed there must be

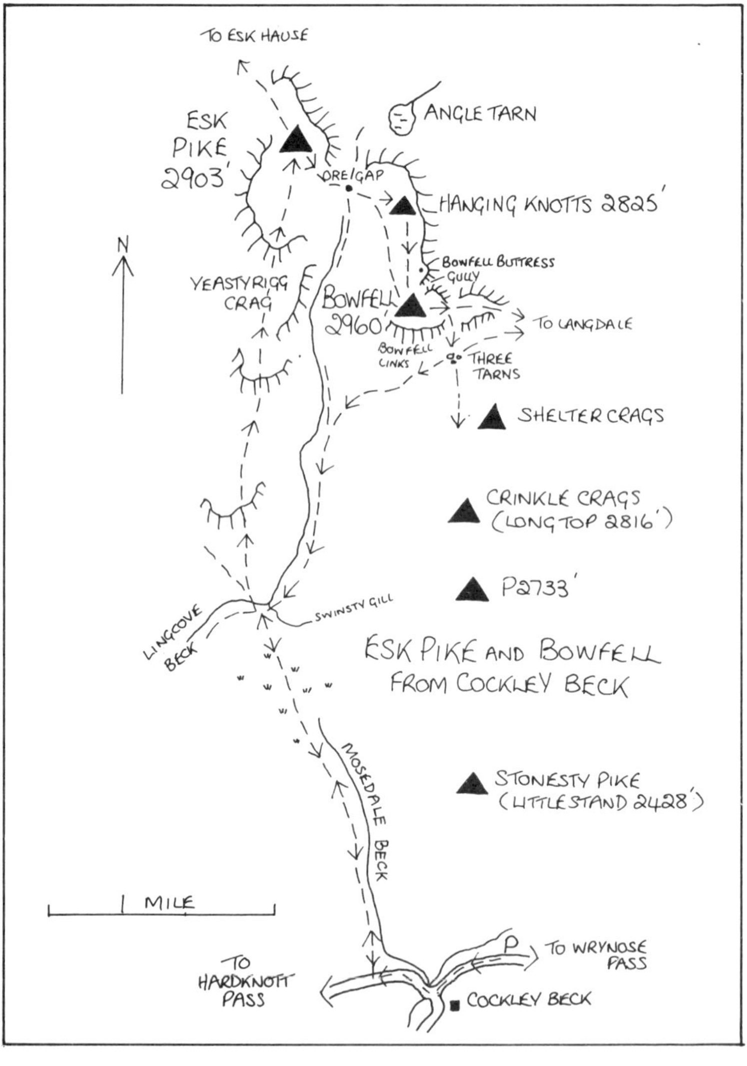

many hundreds of feet of scrambling of varying degrees of difficulty on this ascent, a feature of which is the splendid view leftwards of the craggy Great Moss flanks of Scafell Pike and Ill Crag, cloven apart by the stony stairway of Little Narrowcove.

The ridge follows a north-westerly/north-easterly dog-leg before turning northwards towards the still distant summit. Pike de Bield is the penultimate stony 'burp' before a wide grassy stretch leads up to the outcrops guarding the stony summit dome. It was, of course, named after the famous French climber who made the first ascent of the north face of Loughrigg! An outcrop of pink bulbous rock to the west of the summit provides fun for the scrambler virtually up to the cairn at 2903 feet. There is a stony windbreak below and eastwards of the summit tor should yours be a chilly ascent.

Now descend the well worn path south-easterly into the Ore Gap saddle, so named because the medieval Cistercians packed Eskdale iron ore over it to their 'bloomery' on Smithymire Island in Langstrath. You could at this point, if desired, descend southwards alongside the Yeastyrigg Gill into Lingcove and so back to Cockley Beck. Bowfell looms close, however, and it would be a pity not to 'bag' it whilst you are here. Climb the 'tourist' path but, when it begins to slant right, leave it and head directly eastwards up stony ground to capture the summit of Hanging Knotts, 2825 feet. Now turn right, south, and follow the broad, stony, undulating ridge to rejoin the 'tourist' route beyond the spiky crest of Bowfell Buttress near the grassy lip of a steep gully. In winter, this gully is a popular snow climb, usually crowned by an impressive cornice. In our carefree youth we used to attack it *en masse*, frenziedly wielding our ice axes. We would storm up the gully like a human snow plough, leaving a staircase of armchair-sized steps, a monster bite out of the cornice, and a swirling cloud of spindrift in our wake.

Continue southwards past the gully rim and on up to the spiky tumulus of boulders crowning Bowfell, 2960 feet. Descend eastwards along the terrace above Bowfell Links, then southwards down the wide eroded gully onto the Three Tarns saddle. You now have options open. If you are feeling energetic, continue southwards over Crinkle Crags and Little Stand (Stonesty Pike) before descending steeply south-westerly to Cockley Beck. Or, turn right and follow a path south-westerly down into Lingcove and then down alongside Lingcove Beck to the junction with Swinsty Gill for your final climb back over into Mosedale and down to Cockley Beck.

A Great Langdale Horseshoe

Until the publication, in1980, of Ken Wilson and Richard Gilbert's coffee-table book 'The Big Walks' (though heaven help anyone who spills coffee on my copy), I thought I'd done the Great Langdale Horseshoe many times. I now find that the walk I was accustomed to, from the Old Dungeon Ghyll Hotel over the big peaks around the dalehead and back to the hotel was only for wimps!

Parking: The National Trust car park in Elterwater. (GR 328047).

CROSS the bridge over the Great Langdale Beck and continue on past the Youth Hostel. At the first fork, turn right. At the next fork, turn right, along the tarmac road. Just before a right fork, near a house, turn left into the trees on a path that climbs to the disused Bank Quarry. Here a stile leads on to a path slanting across the fellside to end below a flight of crumbling slate steps leading directly, and interestingly, up into the disused Lingmoor Quarry. In due season both these old quarries are festooned in cushions of Yellow Mountain Saxifrage. Climb steeply left out of Lingmoor Quarry, cross a fence, and join a path heading north-westerly along a broad undulating ridge to reach the Lingmoor cairn.

Continue in the same direction to the right, then to the left, of a wall to reach a stile in a fence below Side Pike. Cross the stile and bear left, below the crag, to an entertaining squeeze behind a rock finger. A 'Fat Man's Agony' as was in the older guidebooks. Turn a corner and scramble up the rocks at the edge of the crag onto the summit of Side Pike and an intimately detailed view of the Langdale Pikes. Descend the south-west ridge to cross the motor road near a cattle grid.

Now follow a path traversing right, across the fellside, to join the popular path up Redacre Gill near where it crosses the beck. Continue steeply up the gill on to easier ground. Easier going now leads to enjoyable scrambling through a belt of rocks, and a final climb up to the slabby summit of Pike O'Blisco, 2304 feet.

Descend south-westerly on to a grassy saddle north of the austere Red Tarn. Climb the steep eroded path up the far slope, passing between Cold Pike and Great Knott, on to easier ground leading to the

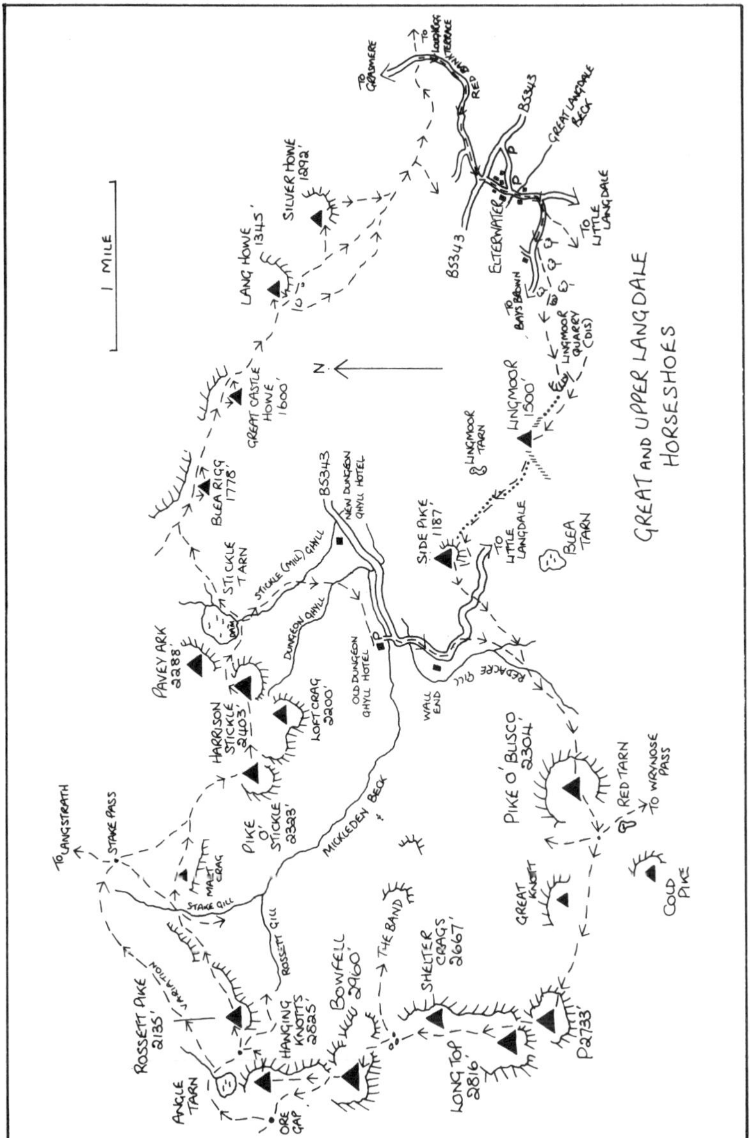

base rocks of Point, 2733 feet. Climb over this first 'crinkle' and down on to a broad saddle. Ahead rises the 'mauvais pas', as real mountain climbers call it, or 'bloody awkward bit' as us fellwalkers say. It's straightforward really. A heave and a couple of steps up the right wall of the gully, below the cave under the huge jammed block, and it's all over. If you don't fancy it,move left from the foot of the gully to find an easier way.

Scramble around the head of the gully then leftwards up to the cairn of Long Top, 2816 feet, the summit of Crinkle Crags. Long Top stands a little west of the main ridge, which runs south-north, so in poor visibility remember this. A lot of people have gone astray here. The rumours that compasses are jinxed on the Crinkles and Bowfell are exaggerated. Keep them well away from the rocks and they will work satisfactorily. A roller-coaster of summits piled with slab and boulder runs north to the Three Tarns saddle below Bowfell. The popular path squirms around the tors wherever possible and avoids completely the separate and easterly-lying summit of Shelter Crags, 2667 feet. My impulse when walking is to keep as strictly to the crests as possible, but this is a long walk, with time and energy of the essence, and my recollection of our attempt is that here we took the easy way. Bowfell offers a rugged challenge ahead, or a threat if you are suffering. The Scafells, breached by the savage cleft of Mickledore, the Great Door, command the north-western skyline. Eastwards, gully and crag fall away into the green, beck-glinty depths of Oxendale.

From Three Tarns a wide eroded gully, to the right of the file of gullies known as Bowfell Links, which can be avoided by pleasant scrambling up the rocks to its right, climbs on to a bouldery ridge. Move left, west, to shortly reach the base of the piled boulders forming the summit of Bowfell, 2960 feet. Descend northwards down the summit blocks and follow cairns to reach the grassy rim of a steep shaly gully below the spiky summit of Bowfell Buttress. This gully is a popular snow climb in winter (see Walk 7). The popular path now slants left across the western flank of Bowfell, down to the Ore Gap. 'The Big Walks' appears to recommend this action, followed by a further drop to Angle Tarn and a traverse across the swampy north-western flank of Rossett Pike to ultimately reach Stake Pass. Given good conditions, I feel it is more interesting to stick to the crests. So, leave the popular path and head northwards, over or around the top of Bowfell Buttress, along a broad, stony, undulating ridge to reach the summit cairn on Hanging Knotts, 2825 feet. Just beyond this cairn and the head of a steep gully, a path turns right down into a hollow. It then slants left down a bouldery terrace into a damp grassy hollow. Descend this, then swing left around a corner, and easy grass then leads down to the eroded path climbing out of Rossett Gill.

Cross this path and climb a ridge curving east on to the summit of Rossett Pike, 2135 feet. Go past the cairn until a cairn overlooking

Langdale is seen ahead. Look left for a faint path heading north-easterly into a hollow running just below the fell crest. Pass below a grassy saddle on to a path slanting down the rocky fellside on to a grassy shelf below Black Crag. Beyond the shelf turn right, down to the bank of Stake Gill where the path to Stake Pass crosses. Pike O'Stickle thrusts its stony cone over the next rise. Follow the path across the beck then turn almost immediately right to climb a fainter path to ultimately reach the cairn and stony blocks crowning Mart Crag. A somewhat swampy path leads around the head of Troughton Beck and up to the short but enjoyable scramble on to the summit of Pike O'Stickle, 2323 feet. Now tramp tiredly eastwards across the boggy hollow of Harrison Combe to capture the apparently truncated summit of Harrison Stickle, 2403 feet. Scramble northwards down the summit rocks before turning east into the hollow between Harrison Stickle and Pavey Ark, where an eroded path leads down on to the shore of Stickle Tarn. Walk right, around the tarn and over the dam to where, just before a beck flows into the tarn, a path climbs right. Follow it, in a north-easterly to easterly direction onto the crest of Blea Rigg and the watershed ridge parting Great Langdale and the Vale of Grasmere.

The purist should now follow this ridge south-easterly, 'bagging' all the many peaklets as he/she goes, to emerge on to the motor road over Red Bank and so back to Elterwater. I have to admit that by this stage I was so 'knackered', if you'll pardon the expression, I was painfully wobbling around, rather than over, the teeniest of hummocks, and the moment I spotted my car parked below on Elterwater Common I hobbled joyfully down towards it.

A comforting feature of this walk is that there are many obvious escape routes, such as the Three Tarns saddle and Rossett Gill, should foul weather or fatigue take their toll.

Walk 9 **12 miles**
5300 feet of ascent

An Upper Langdale Horseshoe

This is the walk I complacently accepted as a Great Langdale Horseshoe until the publication of 'The Big Walks' gave me a rude awakening. Nevertheless, this detracts nothing from its merits as a superb mountain walk. One could argue that it enjoys the cream of the longer walk and that what's left are merely minor summits just added to make the miles up.

Parking: In the large car park to the right of the Old Dungeon Ghyll Hotel, Great Langdale. (GR 286062).

RETURN to the main road and turn right then left along it. Continue with it past the entrance to Wall End Farm to cross a cattle grid near a barn where the road steepens. Beyond the second hairpin look for a path forking right on to the fellside above Redacre Gill. Walk 8 joins in from the left near a beck crossing at the foot of a steep eroded path. Now follow the description in walk 8 from "Continue steeply up the gill on to easier ground" to "where an eroded path leads down on to the shore of Stickle Tarn".

Then, walk around to the dam and turn right down the path alongside Stickle (Mill) Gill. When below the waterfalls look for a path climbing up the right bank alongside a wall. Follow this to eventually go through a kissing-gate and past a seat. Turn right down to a footbridge over Dungeon Ghyll into a walled lane leading back to the Old Dungeon Ghyll Hotel.

Walk 10

Distance varies, depending upon how far you feel like walking after this ascent of Crinkle Crags

Crinkle Crags via Crinkle Gill

The classic walking route over the above peaks is the south-north, or vice versa, traverse of the ridge as per Walks 8 and 9. For those who seek a change, preferably involving a little scrambling, Walks 10 and 11 offer interesting alternatives on to the main ridge.

Parking: As for Walk 9.

WALK back to the road. Turn right to shortly pass through a facing gate and follow the rough track to Stool End Farm. Behind the farm rises the broad ridge known as The Band. Pass through the gate to the left of the farmhouse and follow a path alongside a wall leading into the valley of Oxendale, to the left of The Band. Keep to the path on the right bank of the Oxendale Beck to eventually reach a footbridge at a confluence of gills. Cross the bridge and follow a faint path left into the stony bed of Crinkle Gill.

Soon the walls close in and the scrambling begins. There's one awkward move round a corner with a deep chill pool lying in ambush below. A sharp left turn brings a delightful rock staircase climbing alongside the cascading water. The gill straightens again to a short rock pitch followed by a walk through a spectacular and impending ravine to a waterfall. Now scramble up the grassy right bank towards an archway formed by a detached and leaning rock slab. Climb into and through the archway and scramble on up the gill into an ampitheatre where several becks meet. Go round the base of the central rib and climb a loose shaly groove on its right side to join a path leading left across a grassy ledge above the gill. A final scramble up a rocky rib, or a wet groove to its left, leads on to the open fellside.

Climb steeply up alongside an incipient beck to the left of a small crag. Turn right above the crag then angle left to the base of a scree fan below a steep buttress (cairn). Climb the steep loose scree, or preferably the grassy slopes to its left, to emerge on to the broad saddle below the 'mauvais pas' or 'bloody awkward bit' leading on to Long Top, 2816 feet. This gives a fine, final and scrambly flourish to your ascent.

From Long Top the directions given in Walk 8 or 9 could be followed as far as you desire. Or you could simply amble back down The Band from the Three Tarns.

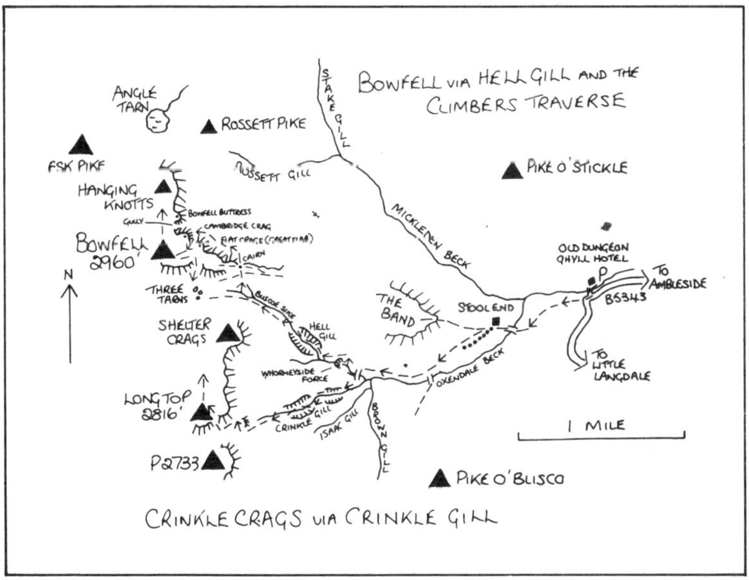

Walk 11 **Distance varies, depending upon how far you feel like walking after this ascent of Bowfell.**

Bowfell via Hell Gill and the Climbers Traverse

Like the previous walk, it gains the crest of a classic ridge by a different approach which has also a flavour of 'mountaineering' about it.

Parking: As for Walk 9.

FOLLOW the directions as for Walk 10 as far as 'a footbridge at a confluence of gills'. Cross the bridge and drop right on to a faint path following the left bank of the beck towards the partially seen Whorneyside Force. On approaching the force, cross over to the right bank to shortly reach a fine pool at the foot of a splendid waterfall. (In dry conditions the fall is climbable, I'm told).

Scramble right up scree than slant left across grassy ledges to reach the top of the fall. I can confirm that a lovely pool above the fall gives a chilly but refreshing 'podgy-dip' on a hot day, should you be so lucky. Continue alongside the beck to reach the entrance to Hell Gill. The impending vegetated walls give it a 'all hope abandon, ye who enter here' look. You can attempt it direct from the first pool or avoid this by a path leading in along the right bank. The scrambling does not last long, leading you into an impressive ampitheatre where the gill forks. Both forks are cul-de-sacs for the scrambler. The dividing spur can be gained by a path on its right side and climbed by earthy ledges onto the open fellside.

Buscoe Sike is the odd name given to the beck spilling into Hell Gill. Cross it to join a path on its far bank and follow it until it begins to swing leftwards towards the Three Tarns saddle. Leave it beyond a fork in the beck and climb north, right, up grass to join an eroded crossing path which is the popular route to Bowfell via The Band. Cross this and climb up steeper and rougher ground to join a higher path on the crest of the ridge. Climb this leftwards, looking for a cairn marking where a narrow path forks right onto the Mickleden flank.

This is the Climbers Traverse. It jinks delightfully across the steep rough fellside to pass below the bulging walls of Flat Crags then on to the foot of a further crag (Cambridge Crag), from the base rocks of which flows a spring of pure chilled water, which is as far as you go. Beyond Cambridge Crag the path crosses a scree gully, which is a popular snow climb in winter (See Walk 7), to end at the foot of the slanting columnar crag of Bowfell Buttress. The climb *Bowfell Buttress*, running centrally up its tilted rocks and one of Lakeland's 'classic' rock climbs, was first climbed in 1902. Now climb left from the spring at the foot of Cambridge Crag up a bouldery path between the crag and the huge slanting roof of Flat Crags, known as the Great Slab. If the rock is dry, move left on to the slab for a more interesting climb. When the crest is reached, climb right to shortly reach the boulder pile forming the summit of Bowfell, 2960 feet.

From Bowfell top the Crinkles beckon you, or finish along routes 8 or 9 as far as you will.

Walk 12 **5 miles**
2500 feet of ascent

The Langdale Pikes via Dungeon Ghyll (Lower Gorge)

These were the first mountains I ever climbed, some thirty seven years ago, and undoubtedly many other mountain folk have that same sentimental affection for them. This walk has some mild scrambling initially, leading into a splendid rocky gorge down which spill a series of lovely off-the-beaten-track waterfalls.

Parking: The free car park, on the right, just beyond the entrance drive to the New Dungeon Ghyll Hotel. (GR 295065).

CLIMB a path through the trees on the left side (west) of the car park to a kissing-gate. Turn left to another kissing-gate. Now climb right, past a seat, to yet another kissing-gate. Descend beyond this to cross the beck and climb the path following its left bank. Shortly, a path and worn rocks drop right into the bed of the ghyll and the entrance to the rock rift into which spills Dungeon Ghyll Force. It's possible to enter the gloomy depths and peer up at the torrent. Climb back out and follow the path up the bank, passing several small cascades. Above them descend a path forking right into the bed of the gill again. Make a zig-zag way up the bed of the gill to round a corner and find a waterfall. Climb steep earthy steps to its right. As soon as possible, move back into the bed of the gill, which now enters a fine rocky gorge. Keep as close to the beck as possible for the best scrambling. Criss-cross several times to eventually emerge into an impressive ampitheatre dominated by a high fall tumbling into a rocky basin. Escape is easier than appearances suggest. A ruddy rock rib on the left leads into a damp gully which leads easily on to the open fellside.

Now cross the beck above the fall and climb up the far bank to join a worn path which ultimately traverses across the steep fellside below the summit rocks of Harrison Stickle and above the depths of the Dungeon Ghyll upper gorge. (A good scramble too, but more serious than the lower gorge). For a stretch above the gorge the path is in a fine position, reminiscent of an alpine path - especially under snow. Emerge from the gorge to join the popular path climbing right, to shortly reach the rocky summit of Harrison Stickle, 2403 feet. The

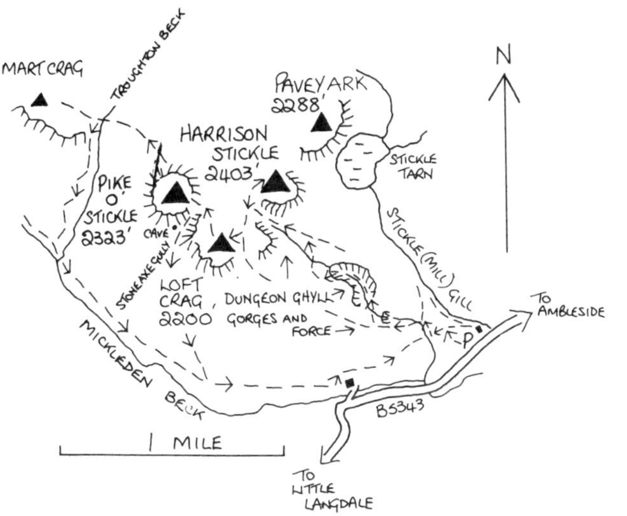

THE LANGDALE PIKES VIA DUNGEON GHYLL (LOWER GORGE)

first recorded ascent of the Langdale Pikes was made in 1797 by Captain Joseph Budworth, a cheerful one-armed veteran of the siege of Gibraltar. On the descent he was overcome by a loss of nerve and a touch of the hyperboles when he came to 'a large bulging part of the mountain, across a sward perpendicular and of immoderate height'. Before he would allow his guide to lead him across this 'mauvais pas' he insisted on bandaging his offside eye with his hankie.

Return the way you came to cross the beck above its fall into the upper gorge, then climb up on to the summit of Loft Crag, 2200 feet. Now head north-west along the rim of the fell to reach the foot of the thrusting rock cone of Pike O'Stickle across the head of a wide steep gully. This gully is known as Stone Axe Gully due to the discovery, in 1947, that a small square-cut cave in its right wall was a 'factory' for the production of Neolithic axe-heads. Since then other 'factories' have been uncovered on Harrison Stickle, Glaramara, Great End and Scafell Pike. Evidently these stone-age fellsmen were not only expert field geologists, but capable of organising a system of production and distribution that saw Lakeland axe-heads exported to a wide area of the British Isles. The rock architecture on both sides of the gully is splendid and the cave lies about a third of the way down. If you wish to see the ‘factory’ descend with care because the gully has become badly eroded by the slithery passage of countless axe-head seekers.

Clamber up an obvious fault line on to the summit of Pike O’Stickle, 2323 feet. Look back for a fine view of the north-west face of Gimmer Crag, scene of many a climbing epic, tucked under the shapely summit of Loft Crag. Descend the summit rocks and if you don’t fancy Stone Axe Gully turn left, north-westerly, along a path descending into the swampy hollow at the head of Troughton Beck. Cross the beck and turn left on a faint path alongside it which improves as it descends in steep zig-zags down onto the eroded track scarring the turfy flats of Mickleden. Turn left and follow this track, passing under the pallid cleft of Stone Axe Gully, eventually to approach a stile at the rear of the Old Dungeon Ghyll Hotel. When close, climb left up the fellside to a higher gate leading into a walled path behind a white house above the hotel. Follow this to a footbridge over Dungeon Ghyll and a junction with your outward route.

EASEDALE

Walk 13 **9 miles**
2300 feet of ascent

Sergeant Man and High Raise via Codale Tarn

The summit of High Raise, or High White Stones as it was more commonly called when I was a mountain mad lad, is a featureless plateau that has little to recommend it. Why bother to climb it, you might ask? Well, it does just scrape into the two thousand five hundred foot contour ring, which puts it into the top sixty fells, depending upon whose list you use to tick your 'peak-bagging'. It also offers widespread views. The real interest in this fell lies in its approaches, however, and that described below is possibly the most interesting.

Parking: The most convenient car park is the one at the entrance to the small housing estate up the Easedale Road. Recently, however, the gas man cometh to Grasmere and is using it to park all his extraneous vans, diggers, etc., upon, leaving limited space. You may have to park in Grasmere, which will make little difference to your legs but some to your pocket. (GR 335079).

WALK up the Easedale Road to where, just before a metal gate, an 'Easedale Tarn' sign points left into a copse of trees where a footbridge spans the Easedale Beck. Cross the bridge, go through a gate, and follow an initially stony path. The cascades of Sour Milk Gill, which drains from Easedale Tarn, can be seen ahead. It is a pleasant approach, well signposted, dominated on either hand by the craggy outlines of Castle Howe and Helm Crag.

The path eventually climbs alongside Sour Milk Gill, then levels, before climbing into the crag-rimmed combe cupping the sombre but tranquil waters of Easedale Tarn. (Recently I've become ashamed of my ignorance of mountain flowers despite nearly forty years of mountain wandering and have made efforts to rectify this. Last summer one of our 'flower-bagging' outings took us to Easedale Tarn and ultimately the summit of Tarn Crag rising above. In boggy patches on the approach to Sour Milk Gill lovely lilac-purply Heath Spotted Orchids and the golden spikes of Bog Asphodel lined our route. Ignoring the path we scrambled up the rocky edges of Sour Milk Gill to find patches of pale Stonecrop and mats of Wild Thyme glistening with spray from the cascades. In the swampy surrounds of the tarn were the insectivores. Common Sundew with their glutinous carmine-fringed 'spoons' invitingly open and, scattered around like stranded starfish, the pale green sticky-leaved rosettes of the Common Butterwort, only a stub of flower remaining in late July, whilst the rocks of the gill we followed to climb Tarn Crag were festooned with cushions of Yellow Mountain Saxifrage.)

Continue with the path along the south bank of the tarn and on past it to climb more steeply alongside Easedale Gill and under the dramatic cone of Belles Knott. When almost opposite the base rocks of Belles Knott look left for a shallow cave at the foot of a crag that is a sheltered spot for a 'breather'. Continue your climb until the path forks. Take the right fork which shortly crosses the beck and swings behind and below the grass slope backing Belles Knott, belying its fierce facade, to shortly reach the shore of tiny Codale Tarn. Walk along the rim of the tarn to follow it left across a feeder beck before climbing a faint cairned path rightwards up the steepish fellside under Lang Crag.

Both path and cairns climb leftwards on to a broad and interesting ramp slanting left below a line of crags and scree fans. Climb the ramp and when it merges into the fellside, continue in the same south-westish line, intermittently cairned, to eventually join the worn path climbing the south-east ridge of Sergeant Man. Below, Stickle Tarn glimmers under the looming profile of Pavey Ark, with Langdale curving away beyond towards Windermere. Turn right to shortly see and soon climb the rocky cone of Sergeant Man, 2414 feet. From here head north-west across the swampy and featureless plateau to reach the windshelter and trig-point crowning High Raise, 2500 feet. The knobbly ridge of Glaramara rises immediately west across the depths of Langstrath, with Gable's proud dome thrusting beyond and Honister Pass an obvious vee-notch rightwards. South-south-westerly, the dark cone of Pike O'Stickle peeks over the plateau rim, with the Coniston fells arrayed behind.

Descend north-easterly from the trig-point to meet stanchions of an old iron fence. Now follow them, plus path, into a dip and up to the summit of Low White Stones. From here the stanchions head north-east down swampy ground on to the saddle of Greenup Edge. In thick mist, rely on your compass, using the intermittent stanchions rather as

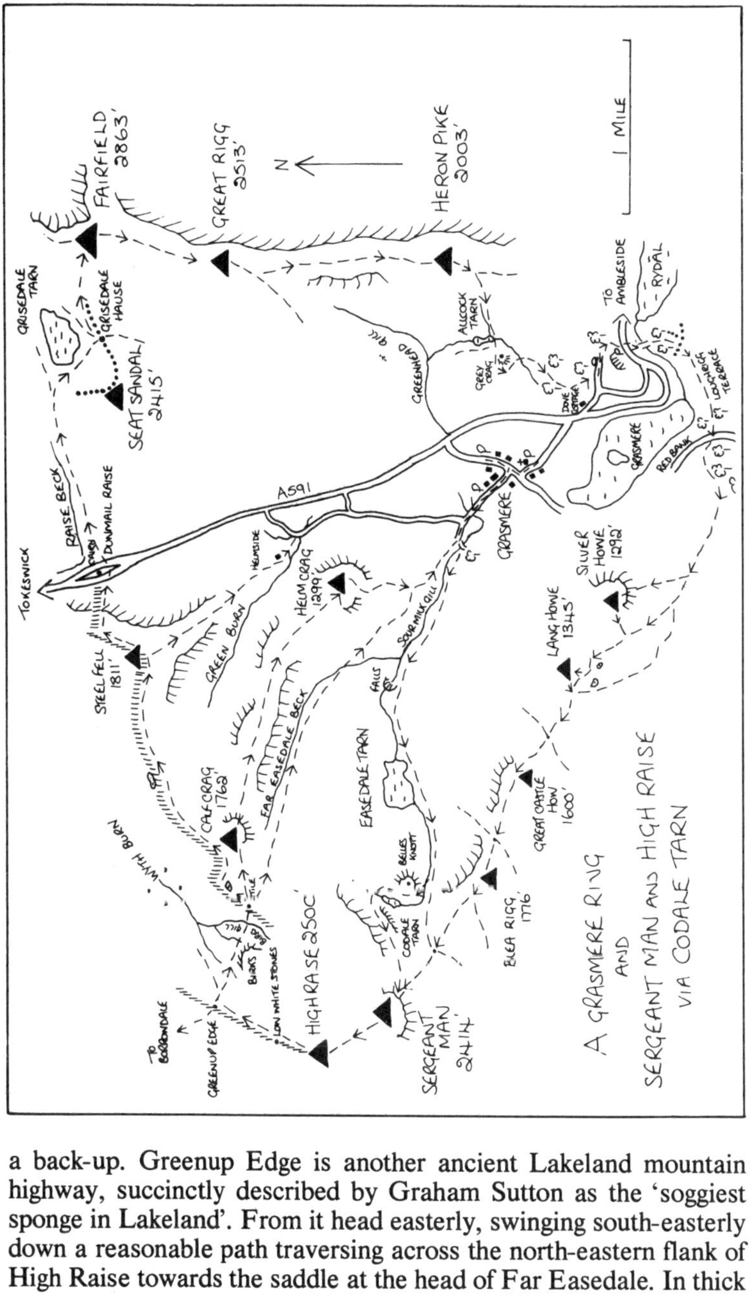

a back-up. Greenup Edge is another ancient Lakeland mountain highway, succinctly described by Graham Sutton as the 'soggiest sponge in Lakeland'. From it head easterly, swinging south-easterly down a reasonable path traversing across the north-eastern flank of High Raise towards the saddle at the head of Far Easedale. In thick mist remember that all the becks here drain north-easterly into the morasses of Wythburn. Do not be tempted to follow one or you will find yourself badly astray and sinking with all hands. The path crosses several becks, passes under crags below Birks, to cross a swampy hollow and Birks Gill before climbing gently to meet the solitary iron stile crowning the saddle at the head of Far Easedale.

Given time and energy there are options open to you here. You can descend directly back to Grasmere down Far Easedale; or climb left on to the summit of Calf Crag and follow the knobbly crest that culminates in Helm Crag; or, and longer, follow the stanchions of an old fence north-easterly behind Calf Crag and in an easterly curve above the lonely valley of Greenburn on to the summit of Steel Fell, before dropping south-easterly back to Grasmere.

Walk 14 — **16 miles**
5100 feet of ascent

A Grasmere Ring

Another, for old me, longer and more strenuous than average day. Done once, for laughs, and never yet repeated. It's a roundabout way of climbing Fairfield, which really has no right to be in this book anyway, but I kind of made it up as I went along. Interesting though.

Parking: In the old quarry used as a car park under White Moss Common, on the A591, near Rydal Water. (GR 348065).

WALK across the road, go down the steps, and walk right to cross the footbridge over the Rothay. Climb up through a wood to a gate in a wall. Go through the gate and turn right to follow the delightful Loughrigg Terrace across the steep north-west flank of Loughrigg to enter a wooded path which leads on to the motor road up Red Bank. Go through a gap in a barrier and cross the road to follow a path climbing rightwards up the far grassy bank. Follow this path around the walled Hammascar Plantation, swinging leftwards to a gate in a wall corner. Beyond, descend into a shallow valley, cross a crossing path, and climb a path up the far slope on to the crest of a ridge.

This broad hummocky ridge forms the watershed between Great Langdale and the Vale of Grasmere. It undulates steadily upward, in a north-westerly direction, to its high point in the rocky cone of Sergeant

Man, 2414 feet, before sinking into the broad featureless plateau culminating in High Raise, 2500 feet. A good path serpentines along the ridge, often avoiding the summits of the peaklets, like Silver Howe, Lang Howe, Great Castle Howe and Blea Rigg, that form its rocky vertebrae. Whether you 'bag' these tops or stick to the main 'trod' depends upon how energetic you are feeling. There are crossing paths, or escape routes, en route, below Little Castle Howe and below and above Blea Rigg. At path forks on Blea Rigg, before the Easedale Tarn-Stickle Tarn crossing, always bear right. Along this ridge have been found 'rough-out' Neolithic axeheads (see Walk 12), suggesting that the Langdale 'factories' packed their wares along this ridge as far as Waterhead for shipment south down Windermere.

Upon reaching Sergeant Man, follow the instructions in Walk 13 from "From here head north-west across the swampy and featureless plateau to reach the windshelter and trig-point crowning High Raise, 2500 feet" to "climbing gently to meet the solitary iron stile crowning the saddle at the end of Far Easedale". Then, climb leftwards up a path alongside occasional rusting old fence stanchions. Shortly, the popular path climbs right on to Calf Crag, from where it follows the knobbly crest that culminates in Helm Crag. You continue with the fence posts, however, passing an unnamed tarn, in a north-easterly /south-easterly dog-leg around Brownrigg Moss, to a fence corner below Calf Crag. Now follow the fenceposts in a north-easterly curve above the lonely valley of Greenburn, passing another substantial unnamed tarn en route, on to the summit of Steel Fell. Here there is a splendid and unique view northwards of Thirlmere.

Descend the north-north-east ridge of Steel Fell alongside a wood and wire fence to where the fence suddenly plunges right, down on to Dunmail Raise. Follow it. It's very steep and rough going initially. I found myself using the fence as a fixed rope, but the angle eases eventually - a bit! By the time you reach the stile leading on to the road you'll feel in the need of urgent knee transplants, you'll be reviling me, and it'll probably be raining. Anyway, the interesting bit's still to come.

Cross the stile, the road, and the stile on the far verge. The ancient cairn crowning the traffic island is reputedly the resting place of one Dunmail, last King of Cumberland, killed in battle here against Saxon invaders. Fact or fiction? Historians say Dunmail died in Rome, with his boots on. Now begin the long climb to Fairfield top. It's only 2076 feet, not a lot if you say it quickly. Initially the climb follows the path alongside Raise Beck to a grassy saddle overlooking Grisedale Tarn. Legend also has it that survivors from the slaughter below fled this way and threw their dead king's regalia into the tarn, out of enemy hands, with their ghosts still repeating the performance. Great story. Appealing to the romantics amongst us. Who but romantics would pursue this daft hobby of mountain climbing? 'Conquistadores of the Useless', the late Lionel Terray entitled his gripping autobiography.

From the saddle, a path traverses right, across the north-east flank of Seat Sandal, to the gap in the old wall crowning Grisedale Hause. Now make the steep climb east, initially alongside the wall, up a steepening and eroded path to eventually emerge on to the stony summit dome of Fairfield, 2863 feet. Descend south-westerly, along the eroded 'Fairfield Horseshoe' path into a dip then up on to the summit of Great Rigg, 2513 feet. Where the ridge forks beyond Great Rigg keep left on the main, narrowing ridge, to eventually climb the twin summits of Heron Pike, 2003 feet. Beyond the second top turn right off the path, and head down the steepish but easy fellside towards Allcock Tarn. Lower down an incipient path, and beck, lead to an iron-barred wall gap. Cross this, and the dam, to descend a good path leftwards close under the spiky summit rocks of Grey Crag. A metal tube set amongst these rocks marks where, every Grasmere Sports day, a flag lures gasping fell runners directly up the steep fellside below - before hurling themselves down again. I have to admit that we 'chickened-out' of Heron Pike. As soon as we saw the tarn glinting below, we slanted straight down the fellside towards it.

A delightful path zig-zags down, with fine views across the Vale of Grasmere of much of the humpety-bumpety skyline over which you have traversed. A last twist left leads to a gate and beyond to a tarmac road. Turn left up this for a final short climb. The tarmac ends near a reedy tarn. To our surprise, for there are dwellings close by, we have disturbed herons on the tarn and deer in the trees across the road. Turn right down a path opposite the tarn shortly to reach the car park.

Walk 15 **7 miles**
2000 feet of ascent

Ullscarf and Launchy Gill

Rising almost slap bang in the middle of mountain Lakeland, Ullscarf could be loosely described as a stowaway Pennine 'pudden'. It is unlikely to figure in most fellwalkers' top twenty Lakeland fells, or even top fifty. Nevertheless, it has many attractions. You are

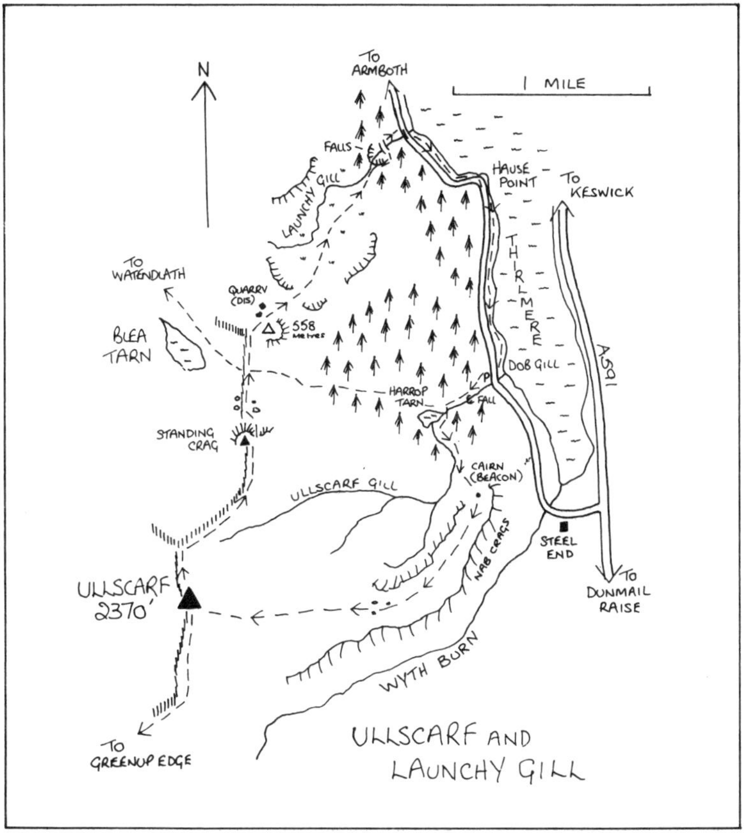

unlikely to meet a crawling centipede of multi-hued cagoules as yet another school party hits the fells; or find coke and beer cans or cigarette packets squashed under the boulder you sit on to eat your sandwiches. You might, however, spot deer, or a fine fox lolloping over the bogs.

Parking: Dob Gill car park on the minor road along the west bank of Thirlmere. (GR 317139).

NOTICES to the effect that deer stalking is in progress and that walkers should keep to the official rights-of-way are displayed in this car park during the shooting season, so best plan the time of your attempt accordingly. Climb the stile in the corner of the car park and climb up through the woods (I've seen red squirrels around here) to emerge on the bank of Dob Gill overlooking a fine waterfall. Continue up through the trees to emerge on the shore of Harrop Tarn where Dob Gill empties from it. Cross the gill by stepping stones and follow the path beyond round to the right to emerge into a clearing split by Ullscarf Gill. To your right, beyond a fence, lies Harrop Tarn. Attracted by the spread of colour we once climbed over this fence to find the swampy tarn banks carpetted in flowering Bogbean, described by William Curtis in his 'Flora Londinensis' as 'one of the most beautiful plants this country can boast'. Turn left and follow the left bank of the beck up through trees to emerge on to the open fellside. Pass above some cascades then look left for a cairn crowning the far skyline, marked 'beacon' on the 2½" map. Climb up to this cairn.

Now head south-south-westerly along the undulating crest of Nab Crags, overlooking the boggy trough of Wythburn. A cluster of exquisite tarnlets are reached where the Wythburn flank veers south-westerly. Now climb more westerly on to the peaty slopes of Ullscarf's broad summit dome to eventually meet the rusty stanchions of the old boundary fence running north to south across the fell, and its companion path. Turn right shortly to reach the cairn. On this section of the walk we once disturbed a fox and watched him hare away down into the boggy basin to our right. Ullscarf - 'the wolf's pass' - has one of Lakeland's most dramatic names blazoned across one of its most undistinguished summits.

Gable, Pillar and Honister Crag feature on the far western skyline. The steep, gill-slashed western flank of Helvellyn can be examined in close-up. It was from Ullscarf I spotted a spoil heap in a nameless gill and subsequently descended it to come upon the workings of the long defunct Helvellyn lead mine.

Descend north-north-westish alongside the stanchions to meet the corner of a recently erected wood and wire fence. Turn right and, keeping this fence to your left, follow it to its end on the lip of Standing Crag. Below, Blea Tarn points like an assegai blade towards Bassenthwaite Lake and the far gleam of the Solway. An expatriate Londoner I brought this way wouldn't believe that a faint line of hills was Scotland. He'd heard of it, but thought it started nearer the Arctic Circle! Turn right and scramble down the rocks behind the rim of the crag before descending left into a grassy groove to rejoin the fence close to the foot of the crag. (Recently I sat with friends on the rocks above the crag when a fox popped out of the grassy groove - to our delight and his/her consternation).

Follow the fence over swampy ground, past a couple of shallow tarns, to meet the Watendlath-Thirlmere path by a gate. The medieval Cistercian monks of Furness Abbey had this right-of-way to pack produce from their Borrowdale holdings. Cross this path and continue with the fence until it veers left. Leave it here and climb north-east over a ridge to the left of a rocky eminence marked 558 metres. Descend the far slope to find a surprisingly large ruin (quarry) near evident excavation. Continue on to see spread below a great swampy bowl through which wends Launchy Gill. Your target is the tree-fringed mouth of the bowl where the gill begins its long and spectacular fall into Thirlmere. Pick your way down into the bowl and skirt around its right-hand edge where you will find a surprising amount of firm ground. We have disturbed deer browsing here, and landrover tracks crossing the bowl and a newish wooden hut (hide?) perched high to the right are probable results of stalking.

Climb over the fence into the trees to find a path traversing right. Follow it a little way to a fine viewpoint down on to Thirlmere. Now head back towards the sound of falling water. There is no definite path but it is possible with care to scramble down the steep right bank of the gill and get close-quarter views of a succession of superb cascades. Eventually a 'tourist' path will be met leading on to a footbridge spanning the gill. We recently crossed this bridge on a day when four inches of rain fell upon Keswick. The gill was wall to wall an unbroken torrent of thundering white water that set the bridge of a tremble under our feet. Spray rose like smoke above the trees.

Cross the bridge and follow the path down the far bank, alongside yet more cascades, to reach the road. Follow the road back across the gill then turn left through a gate. Now follow the path along the lakeshore for just over a very pleasant mile, emerging briefly onto the road again at the Hause Point viewpoint, to where Dob Gill empties into the lake. Turn right here over a boggy area to reach a gate leading on to the road opposite the car park.